Britain and
Hong Kong

D1612804

London: H M S O

Researched and written by Reference Services, Central Office of Information

This publication is an expanded and updated version of a fact sheet with the same title previously published for the Foreign & Commonwealth Office

HMSO publications are available from:

HMSO Publications Centre
(Mail, fax and telephone orders only)
PO Box 276, London SW8 5DT
Telephone orders 071-873 9090
General enquiries 071-873 0011
(queing system in operation for both numbers)

HMSO Bookshops
49 High Holborn, London WC1V 6HB 071-873 0011
Fax 071-873 8200 (counter service only)
258 Broad Street, Birmingham B1 2HE 021-643 3740 Fax 021-643 6510
Southey House, 33 Wine Street, Bristol BS1 2BQ
0272 264306 Fax 0272 294515
9-21 Princess Street, Manchester M60 8AS 061-834 7201 Fax 061-833 0634
16 Arthur Street, Belfast BT1 4GD 0232 238451 Fax 0232 235401
71 Lothian Road, Edinburgh, EH3 9AZ 031-228 4181 Fax 031-229 2734

HMSO's Accredited Agents
(see Yellow Pages)

and through good booksellers

Photo Credits
Numbers refer to the pages in the illustration section (1–4):
Alan Symes p. 1 (top), p. 3 (bottom), p. 4; R. Henbury p. 1 (bottom), p. 3 (top).

[Front cover] Hong Kong's Central District.

Contents

Introduction

This booklet describes Britain's policy towards Hong Kong, including progress towards implementation of the 1984 Sino-British Joint Declaration. It also contains the complete text of the declaration and provides background information on Hong Kong's political, economic and social development. There is also a map of the territory.

With a population of just over 5·8 million, Hong Kong is situated on the south-east coast of the People's Republic of China. The land area is 1,074 sq km (415 square miles) and the overall population density is 5,385 per sq km.

Under the Treaty of Nanjing (1842) and the first Convention of Peking (1860), Hong Kong Island, the southern part of the Kowloon Peninsula and Stonecutters Island were ceded to Britain in perpetuity. The rest of the territory was ceded to Britain for 99 years from 1 July 1898 under the 1898 Convention of Peking; consisting of the area north of Kowloon up to the Shenzhen River and 235 adjacent islands, it is known as the New Territories.

The Chinese Government has consistently taken the view that the whole of Hong Kong is Chinese territory. Its position for many years was that the question of Hong Kong came into the category of unequal treaties left over from history. It has always sought to settle the matter through negotiations when conditions were ripe and has maintained the status quo pending a settlement.

The Joint Declaration

Negotiation of the Joint Declaration

The expiry of the New Territories' lease on 30 June 1997 made it necessary to tackle the question of Hong Kong's future, since the remaining 8 per cent of Hong Kong's land area is not viable without the New Territories, which contain most of the agriculture and industry, the power stations, the airport and the container port. Moreover, by the late 1970s, concern about the future had grown, both locally and among foreign investors. A particular problem was the inability of the Hong Kong Government to grant new leases in the New Territories extending beyond 1997.

The British Government concluded that there was a need to remove the uncertainty created by the 1997 deadline, and in 1982 discussions were opened with the Chinese Government during a visit of the then Prime Minister, Mrs Margaret Thatcher, to Peking. A statement issued by both sides on 24 September 1982 said that agreement had been reached to enter talks through diplomatic channels 'with the common aim of maintaining the stability and prosperity of Hong Kong'.

During the talks with the Chinese Government, the British side initially argued for the retention of British administration as the surest way of maintaining Hong Kong's prosperity and stability. After long discussions, it became clear that the continuation of British administration was unacceptable to the Chinese Government and that the only way forward was to negotiate alternative arrangements which would secure a high degree of autonomy for Hong Kong and enable it, as a Special Administrative Region (SAR) of China, to preserve its existing way of life and the essential elements of its present system. After intensive negotiations, the Joint Declaration—embodying the concept of one country, two systems—was initialled by Britain and China on 26 September 1984 (see Appendix for the complete text).

When the Joint Declaration was published, the British Government said that it provided 'the necessary assurances about Hong Kong's future which will allow the territory to continue to flourish, and to maintain its unique role in the world as a major trading and financial centre'. The choice, imposed by the facts of Hong Kong's history, was between reversion of Hong Kong to China under agreed legally binding international arrangements or reversion to China without such arrangements. The British Government therefore commended the agreement to the people of Hong Kong and to the British Parliament.

Following publication of the Joint Declaration, the views of the people of Hong Kong were collected and analysed by an Assessment Office appointed by the Hong Kong Government. In November 1984 the Office reported that most people found the draft to be acceptable. The Joint Declaration was then approved by the British Parliament and signed by Britain and China on 19 December 1984. It entered into force on 27 May 1985, when instruments of ratification were exchanged in Peking between the British and Chinese Governments. On 12 June it was registered at the United Nations by the two Governments in accordance with normal practice. The Joint Declaration was widely welcomed internationally as a major diplomatic achievement.

Contents of the Joint Declaration

The Joint Declaration was concluded because of a unique set of circumstances. Unlike other British dependent territories, where British policy has been to prepare them for independence, the 1898 Convention of Peking and other factors made it necessary to make arrangements for Hong Kong's return to Chinese sovereignty. In recognition of its responsibility to the people of Hong Kong, the British Government has tried to ensure that this change takes place in such a way as to preserve the way of life, prosperity and stability of the territory.

The Joint Declaration is designed to achieve this; paragraph 7 stipulates that the two governments agree to implement the Joint Declaration and three annexes, the first of which describes in detail Chinese policies towards Hong Kong after 1997. The paragraph has the effect of making them legally binding on both parties. The main provisions are as follows:

—China will enact a Basic Law stipulating that the socialist system and socialist policies will not be practised in the Hong Kong SAR and that Hong Kong's capitalist system and life style will remain unchanged for 50 years.

—Except in relation to foreign affairs and defence, the Hong Kong SAR will enjoy a high degree of autonomy, including executive, legislative and independent judicial power.

—The government and legislature of the Hong Kong SAR will be composed of local inhabitants. The Chief Executive will be selected by election or through consultations held locally and will be appointed by the Chinese Government.

—The legislature will be constituted by elections. The executive authorities will be required to act in accordance with the law and will be accountable to the legislature.

—The Hong Kong SAR will have its own legal system and laws after 1997. The laws will include those previously in force before 1997 and laws passed by the SAR legislature, provided that they do not contravene the Basic Law.

—The judicial system in Hong Kong will remain essentially unchanged. Hong Kong will have its own Court of Final Appeal. The independence of the judiciary and the prosecuting authority will be maintained.

—There will be continuity in the public service and serving officers will be able to continue after 1997 on terms and conditions no less favourable than before.

—The SAR Government will determine its own fiscal policy. There will be no requirement to remit revenue to the Chinese Government. The present systems of accountability to the legislature for all public expenditure and impartial auditing of accounts will be retained.

—Hong Kong will continue to determine its economic and trade policies. Its free enterprise system will continue and it will retain its role as a free port.

—Hong Kong will continue to have a freely convertible currency. The Hong Kong SAR will manage the Exchange Fund (see p. 37), which provides the backing for the note issue and is used to regulate the exchange value of the currency.

—Hong Kong will retain its position as a major shipping centre and have its own shipping register. Merchant shipping will have free access to Hong Kong ports.

—All scheduled air services touching the Hong Kong SAR will be regulated by separate agreements concluded by the SAR Government. Hong Kong will enjoy autonomy in many civil aviation matters, for example, licensing local airlines and maintaining its own aircraft register.

—While defence and foreign affairs will be the responsibility of the Chinese central government, the Hong Kong SAR will manage certain aspects of its external relations; it will be able to negotiate agreements and participate in appropriate international organisations. There will be continuity of representation by foreign states and organisations currently represented in Hong Kong, subject to the approval of the Chinese central government.

—Maintenance of law and order will be the responsibility of the SAR Government. Chinese military forces stationed in Hong Kong will not interfere in the SAR's internal affairs.

—Protection under the law against infringements of rights and freedoms will be maintained. The provisions of the International Covenants on Civil and Political Rights and on Economic, Social and Cultural Rights, as applied to Hong Kong, will continue to apply to the SAR.

—The right of people to leave Hong Kong for any purpose, such as business, study or emigration, will be maintained.

Implementation of the Joint Declaration

Relations with China

The British Government has always attached importance to maintaining close and friendly relations with China in the belief that this is in Hong Kong's interests. Although the confidence of Hong Kong was seriously shaken by the events of June 1989 in Peking, and Sino-British relations suffered an inevitable setback, the British Government remains committed to the Joint Declaration. In a report published in June 1989, the House of Commons Foreign Affairs Committee described it as 'the best and surest treaty base for the future of Hong Kong', a view shared by political opinion in the territory.

The Chinese Government has also repeatedly reaffirmed its intention to honour its obligations under the Joint Declaration and its commitment to the policy of 'one country, two systems'. China has a substantial stake in Hong Kong's continuing success. Hong Kong provides one-third of China's foreign exchange earnings and two-thirds of its foreign investment; it is also China's largest international trading partner and its gateway to the international trading system.

In September 1991 Britain and China signed a Memorandum of Understanding confirming their wish to intensify their co-operation over Hong Kong in accordance with the Joint Declaration. Both sides agreed that their two foreign ministers should meet twice a year to discuss Hong Kong and other questions. Regular meetings also take place between the Governor of Hong Kong and Chinese officials.

The Basic Law

The Basic Law gives legal effect under the Chinese constitution to the provisions of the Joint Declaration. It is a Chinese law drafted by a committee appointed by the Chinese authorities but including a number of Hong Kong representatives among its members. The drafting committee was assisted by a consultative committee in Hong Kong, also appointed by the Chinese Government, with the task of finding out the views of Hong Kong people on the draft of the Basic Law.

The first draft was published in April 1988. After a period of consultation in Hong Kong, and subsequent revisions, a second draft was published in February 1989 for another round of public consultation. The final draft was published in February 1990. It was enacted and promulgated by the National People's Congress in April 1990.

The Basic Law is the product of extensive consultations conducted with the Hong Kong people over a period of five years by the Chinese authorities. The British Government has taken a very close interest in this process and has made its views known to the Chinese Government. Its concern throughout was to ensure consistency between the Basic Law and the provisions of the Joint Declaration. As a result of the consultation process, and in response to the British Government's detailed representations, a number of changes were made in the final version. In Britain's view the Basic Law provides a satisfactory basis for Hong Kong's future status as a part of China with a high degree of autonomy.

Sino-British Liaison Group

Implementation of the Joint Declaration is the task of the Sino-British Liaison Group established under it. It discusses matters related to the smooth transfer of government in 1997 and exchanges information. The Group plays no part in Hong Kong's administration.

The Group comprises a senior representative and four other members on each side. Supporting staff and experts also attend meetings as appropriate. Both sides have offices in Hong Kong and their senior representatives are resident in the territory, thereby facilitating closer contacts. The Group is required to hold plenary sessions at least three times a year, meeting sequentially in Peking, London and Hong Kong. The Group will remain in existence until 1 January 2000, which means that the British Government will be in a position for two and half years after 1997 to monitor and influence the implementation of the Joint Declaration.

The Group has concluded agreements on:

—Hong Kong's new status as a separate contracting party to the General Agreement on Tariffs and Trade (GATT). Hong Kong became GATT's ninety-first contracting party in April 1986 and will retain that status after 1997 in the name of 'Hong Kong, China'.

—Hong Kong's participation after 1997 in over 26 international organisations, including the International Monetary Fund, the World Bank, the Asian Development Bank, the International Telecommunications Satellite Organisation and the International Maritime Satellite Organisation.

—The establishment of Hong Kong's own Air Services Agreements capable of remaining in force after 1997; agreements have been signed with Brazil, Brunei, Canada, France, Malaysia, the Netherlands, New Zealand and Switzerland.

—The expansion of the police force to enable it to take full responsibility for the maintenance of public order, including duties currently undertaken by British forces to combat illegal immigration.

—Transitional arrangements for the different types of travel and identity documents used by Hong Kong people to avoid any disruption on 1 July 1997.

—A wide variety of legal matters, including the replacement of English laws by local legislation in a form which can continue after 1997.

Land Commission

The Sino-British Land Commission was established in 1985 in accordance with Annex III to the Joint Declaration. Its purpose is to consult on the implementation of provisions on land leases and other related matters. The Commission is composed of three officials from each side and meetings are held in Hong Kong.

Under Annex III, premium income from land transactions, after deduction of the average cost of land reclamation, clearance and other related costs, is shared between the Hong Kong Government and the future SAR Government. The Hong Kong Government's share of the premium income is put into the Capital Works Reserve Fund for financing public works and land development. The future SAR Government's share is held in a trust fund established by the Chinese side of the Commission; this fund is managed under the direction and advice of an investment committee which includes prominent Hong Kong bankers, as well as a monetary expert from the Hong Kong Government. Nearly HK$20,000 million has been transferred to the trust fund.

History

Hong Kong was inhabited from prehistoric times, but remained sparsely populated up to the nineteenth century. The oldest villages have a history of continuous settlement dating back to the eleventh century.

The Guangdong area of the Chinese mainland was first brought under the suzerainty of China between 221 and 214 BC, although Chinese migration on a large scale did not come until the Song (Sung) Dynasty (AD 960–1279). British attempts during the seventeenth century to establish trade with China were unsuccessful, but the volume of trade between the two countries grew rapidly during the eighteenth century, Britain becoming the leading commercial power in the China seas.

The development of trading relations was for long resisted by the officials of the Chinese court, who were not interested in commercial or cultural relations with Western civilisation, which they regarded as inferior to their own. In 1757 European traders were confined to Guangzhou (Canton), where the merchants found Chinese laws and the way they were administered troublesome and where they were subject to many personal restrictions. A conflict occurred in the period from 1839 to 1842, when a British force occupied Guangzhou and other points after a Chinese attempt to enforce the laws against the profitable opium trade which supplied the West's principal means of payment for Chinese goods.

By the 1841 Convention of Chuanbi, Hong Kong Island, then little more than a barren rock, was ceded to Britain and formally occupied in January 1841. The British and Chinese Governments, however, were dissatisfied with this agreement and refused to ratify it. Hostilities were resumed and were ended in 1842 by the Treaty of Nanjing, recognising the cession in perpetuity of the island to Britain.

The Convention of Peking, concluded in 1860 after further hostilities between Britain and China, secured the cession to Britain of part of Kowloon and Stonecutters Island. Hong Kong's boundaries were extended in 1898 by another Convention of Peking, which authorised a 99-year lease of the New Territories to Britain.

Hong Kong suffered a series of setbacks in its early years from fire, disease and typhoons but became a centre of Chinese emigration and trade with Chinese communities abroad and a depot for European and American merchants.

Public and utility services developed in response to increasing population, trade and business—a gas company in 1861, a tramway in 1885, an electricity supply company in 1903, electric tramways in 1904 and the Kowloon–Canton railway, which was completed in 1910. A system of public education began in 1847 with grants to Chinese vernacular schools and in 1873 voluntary schools mainly run by missionaries were included in a grant scheme. The College of Medicine for the Chinese, founded in 1887, developed into the University of Hong Kong in 1911. Development also took place in housing, sanitation and water conservation to meet the needs of the ever-growing population.

From the beginning, free access to Hong Kong was given to the Chinese population from the mainland and on several occasions refugees fled to the territory. During the Taiping rebellion which broke out in 1850, thousands sought refuge in Hong Kong; similarly, after the overthrow of the Manchu dynasty in 1911 there was a long period of unrest in China during which large numbers of people found shelter in Hong Kong. The population rose from 32,983 (31,463 Chinese) in 1851 to 878,947 (859,425 Chinese) in 1931. During the Japanese invasion of China between 1937 and 1939 about 750,000 refugees brought the population to about 1·6 million in 1939.

In December 1941 Japan attacked Hong Kong from the mainland, the British being forced to retire to Hong Kong Island. After surrendering on Christmas Day, the territory was occupied for three years and seven months. Its life was seriously disrupted during this period and the population decreased.

When Japan surrendered in 1945 a provisional government was set up in Hong Kong. Civil government was formally restored in May 1946. Chinese civilians returned to the territory, the population rising to about 1·8 million by the end of 1947. Because of the arrival of refugees from the Chinese civil war, which culminated in the victory of the Chinese Communists in 1949, the population was an estimated 2·3 million by the end of 1950. This growing population pressure obliged the Hong Kong Government to impose restrictions for the first time on the entry of Chinese from the mainland, although tens of thousands continued to gain entry illegally. In October 1980 new legislation provided for the repatriation of illegal immigrants.

After a period of economic stagnation caused by the United Nations embargo on trade with China following the outbreak of the Korean war in 1950, massive industrial expansion in the Hong Kong economy occurred; this enabled increased government spending to take place on education, health, housing and social welfare programmes.

Government and Administration

Constitutional Development

The system of government in Hong Kong reflects the territory's circumstances. In other British dependent territories, the development of democracy has been promoted as part of the preparations for eventual independence. Different considerations have applied in the case of Hong Kong.

After the second world war (1939–45), Hong Kong was preoccupied with absorbing and accommodating large numbers of immigrants, mainly from China, and with adjusting to the loss of its entrepôt trade with China as a result of the Korean War in the early 1950s. The priority for much of the population was that Hong Kong should be an environment in which people could settle and make a prosperous living, rather than develop representative government. A further consideration, to which many members of the community attached particular weight, was the fear that the introduction of party politics would reproduce the political rivalries between Chinese Communists and Nationalists which could have had a seriously destabilising effect on the territory. Local attitudes were also influenced by the desire not to upset the conditions which permitted Hong Kong to continue to exist as an enclave on the coast of China.

The Hong Kong Government therefore sought consensus through an extensive network of consultation boards and committees (now over 400) which enable the public to give their views on all areas of government activity. As the population became increasingly settled, care was taken to ensure that this system evolved to meet the requirements and aspirations of the people, while maintaining social stability, effective administration and economic prosperity.

In the 1970s the Legislative Council was expanded to include more members who were not officials of the administration, but all Council members were still appointed. In 1985 provision was made for 24 members to be indirectly elected from local government bodies and functional constituencies based on major professional and occupational groups. In 1991, 18 directly elected seats were introduced. The final version of the Basic Law provides for the number of directly elected seats to rise to 24 in 1999 and 30 (50 per cent) in 2003, with the possibility that full direct elections could be introduced in 2007. The British Government hopes that in time the Chinese Government will agree to accelerate the pace of democratisation.

In the 1980s elected members were introduced in the Urban and Regional Councils and local District Boards (see p. 20).

Central Government

Hong Kong is administered by the Hong Kong Government, headed by the Governor, who is appointed by the Queen. The Governor presides over the Executive Council—the principal decision-taking body—and the Legislative Council, which passes laws and authorises public expenditure. He has ultimate direction of the administration and is the titular Commander-in-Chief of the British forces stationed in Hong Kong. There are two municipal councils responsible for local government.

Because of Hong Kong's status as a dependent territory, foreign relations are constitutionally the direct responsibility of the British Government, although the territory has a high degree of autonomy on issues like trade. On virtually all internal matters, Hong Kong is left to conduct its own affairs; in practice the Governor rarely exercises his formal powers to their full extent. Hong Kong is governed by consent and by consultations with the community.

Executive Council

On policy matters the Governor acts in accordance with the advice of the Executive Council, which is made up of four ex-officio members—the Chief Secretary, the Commander British Forces, the Financial Secretary and the Attorney-General—together with ten other members appointed by the Governor with the approval of the Foreign and Commonwealth Secretary.

The Executive Council plays a role similar to that fulfilled by the Cabinet in Britain. It normally meets once a week and its proceedings are confidential, although many of its decisions are made public. The Governor is required to consult the Council on all important matters of policy, and decisions are made by consensus. The Governor-in-Council—the Governor acting in consultation with the Executive Council—is Hong Kong's central and most important executive authority. In addition to policy matters, the Governor-in-Council decides appeals, petitions and objections under those ordinances which confer a statutory right of appeal.

The Executive Council considers all principal legislation before it is introduced in the Legislative Council and is responsible for making subsidiary legislation under a number of ordinances.

Legislative Council

The Legislative Council consists of the Governor, who is the President, three ex-officio members (the Chief Secretary, the Financial Secretary and the Attorney General), 18 members appointed by the Governor and 18 members directly elected from geographical constituencies. In addition, there are 21 members elected from functional constituencies representing occupational or professional groups. Each of the two municipal councils is also a functional constituency.

The Council meets in public once a week. Members may address it in Chinese or English, simultaneous interpretation being provided. Legislation is enacted in the form of Bills which go through three readings and a committee stage. There are also two major debates in each session—one on government policy, which follows the Governor's address at the opening of the session in October each year, and the other on the budget, which takes place in March. Members may also question the Hong Kong Government on policy issues, either to seek information or ask for official action. A verbatim record of proceedings is kept.

The Council's Finance Committee scrutinises all proposals for public expenditure and its authority is required for any changes made to the annual appropriations approved by the Legislative Council. The Public Accounts Committee examines and reports on the findings in the annual report of the Director of Audit, as well as reports made by the Director on value-for-money studies undertaken by him. Both committees meet in public, although the Finance Committee occasionally considers individual cases in private.

A new committee structure was introduced in 1992 in the form of ten formal bills committees to scrutinise draft legislation.

OMELCO

The non-official members of the Executive and Legislative Councils have their own staff and offices in the form of the Office of Members of the Executive and Legislative Councils. They have set up specialist panels to monitor the policy and progress of work in the various areas of government activity, such as education, health, welfare, the Civil Service, transport, trade, industry and security. These panels meet regularly with senior civil servants to discuss policy proposals. The non-official members of the Legislative Council also form ad hoc groups to examine Bills introduced into the Council. Much of the detailed discussion of Bills takes place in meetings between these groups and the relevant policy branches of the Government. Amendments are frequently negotiated and agreed and subsequently introduced into the Council during the committee stage.

OMELCO established a London office in April 1990.

Local Government

The Urban and Regional Councils are responsible for providing municipal services to the population in urban areas and the New Territories respectively. These include street cleaning and refuse collection, food hygiene, liquor licensing, provision of sports facilities and the management of museums, libraries and other cultural institutions. The Councils are statutory bodies and are financially autonomous. Their major source of income is from fees, charges and rates collected in their area.

The Urban Council consists of 40 councillors—15 directly elected from district constituencies, 15 appointed by the Governor and one representative member from each of the ten urban District Boards. There are 36 members of the Regional Council—

12 are directly elected, nine represent the other District Boards and 12 are appointed by the Governor. Its three ex-officio members are the Chairman and two Vice-Chairmen of the Heung Yee Kuk, a statutory advisory body representing the indigenous population of the New Territories.

The 19 District Boards are statutory bodies providing a forum for public consultation and participation. They have a mainly advisory role with substantial responsibility for the management of district affairs. In monitoring the Hong Kong Government's performance, they discuss a wide range of matters affecting residents. The Boards receive some public funds for local recreational and cultural activities and for minor environmental work. They have 274 elected and 140 appointed members.

The Administration

The Chief Secretary advises the Governor on policy and, as head of the Government Secretariat, is responsible for its implementation. The Financial Secretary is responsible for fiscal and economic policies and lays before the legislature the Hong Kong Government's annual estimates of revenue and expenditure. The Attorney-General is the Government's legal adviser, is responsible for drafting legislation and has independent responsibility for the conduct of prosecutions.

The Hong Kong public service, including the police, employs about 180,000 staff, 98 per cent of which are local officers.

The Office of the Commissioner for Administrative Complaints investigates, and reports on, grievances arising from administrative decisions, acts and recommendations. The Office has independent jurisdiction over all government departments except the police and the Independent Commission Against Corruption. The Commissioner makes an annual report to the Governor.

The Legal System

The legal system is based on that in England and Wales. Statutory law is created by ordinances which generally follow the principle of English Acts of Parliament. The Hong Kong Government has adopted a programme to replace English laws applying to Hong Kong by local ordinances; this is being done to ensure that by 1997 the territory has a comprehensive body of law owing its authority to the Hong Kong legislature. The Hong Kong Act 1985, passed by the British Parliament, gave the legislature the powers to implement this programme.

The judiciary is independent from the executive and legislative branches of government. The most senior court in Hong Kong is the Supreme Court, comprising the Court of Appeal and the High Court. Sitting in the Supreme Court are the Chief Justice, who is the head of the judiciary, nine Justices of Appeal and 20 High Court judges. The Registrar, Deputy Registrars and Assistant Registrars also have jurisdiction as Masters of the Supreme Court in civil trials in the High Court.

The High Court's jurisdiction is unlimited in civil and criminal matters. The Court's judges usually sit alone when trying civil matters and, for criminal trials, with a jury of seven (or nine, on special direction of the judge); the issue of guilt in criminal trials is determined by the jury, which must have a majority of at least five to two.

Below the High Court is the District Court, which also has civil and criminal jurisdiction; the former is limited to disputes not exceeding a value of HK$120,000 and the latter to offences carrying a sentence of up to seven years' imprisonment.

Some 90 per cent of all the cases heard in the territory are tried in the Magistrates' Courts, which have a purely criminal jurisdiction and which can impose a maximum of two years' imprisonment and a fine of up to HK$10,000. There are 60 professional magistrates.

Professional magistrates also try cases in the Juvenile Court, which has jurisdiction regarding charges made against children and young people up to the age of 16 years, except in cases involving homicide.

The Court of Appeal hears civil and criminal appeals from the High Court and the District Court. Further appeal is possible to the Judicial Committee of the Privy Council in London, although this is infrequent, as leave to appeal is granted only on stringent conditions of public interest. Draft legislation is currently being prepared to set up before 1997 a local Court of Appeal to take over the role of the Privy Council in Hong Kong.

There are five specialised tribunals dealing with small claims, land disputes, contracts of employment, obscene articles and unusual circumstances.

There is a legal aid scheme to help people who are unable to meet the costs of legal action. Free legal advice is also available to people who cannot afford to consult private lawyers.

Bill of Rights
The International Covenants on Civil and Political Rights and on Economic, Social and Cultural Rights have applied in Hong Kong since 1976. The Joint Declaration provides for their continued application beyond 1997.

Because of local support for these freedoms to be embodied in a Bill of Rights, legislation has been passed giving effect in local law to the International Covenant on Civil and Political Rights. This provides for legal redress in the courts if anyone believes that his or her civil or political rights, as defined in the Covenant, have been violated. The Hong Kong Government seeks to implement the other Covenant through existing legislation and policies.

Public Order

The Royal Hong Kong Police Force, formed in 1842, has an establishment of over 27,500 and a civilian staff of nearly 6,000. It is trained and led by British and Chinese officers and the lower ranks are almost entirely Chinese in composition. The Force should be predominantly staffed by local officers by the year 2000. At present overseas officers constitute about 60 per cent at the rank of superintendent and above, while three-quarters of inspectors are local officers. Steps are being taken to identify more local officers for promotion and to provide training to develop their potential.

The Force is responsible for crime prevention and detection, the maintenance of public order, anti-drug operations and combating illegal immigration from China.

The Complaints Against Police Office investigates all complaints from the public about the conduct and behaviour of members of the police force. Investigation of complaints against police officers is monitored by the Police Complaints Committee, an independent body appointed by the Governor; its chairman and two vice-chairmen are drawn from OMELCO.

Independent Commission Against Corruption

The Independent Commission Against Corruption was set up in 1974 to investigate suspected cases of corruption, to advise on ways of reducing opportunities for corruption and to inform the public about its dangers. The Commissioner is directly responsible to the Governor.

Defence

The British garrison assists the Hong Kong Government in maintaining the territory's stability and security. It currently consists of four infantry battalions with supporting units, a Royal Air Force helicopter squadron and Royal Navy patrol craft. This garrison is gradually being withdrawn in the period leading up to 1997. During the course of 1992 one battalion is being withdrawn.

Hong Kong contributes 65 per cent of the garrison's running costs and the British Government 35 per cent. Hong Kong's financial contribution is determined by the Defence Costs Agreement between Hong Kong and Britain. The current agreement was renegotiated in 1988 in terms that will last until the garrison's departure. Under this agreement the future size and composition of the garrison is subject to regular consultation between the two Governments.

There are two locally recruited auxiliary services—the Royal Hong Kong Regiment (The Volunteers), which is a light reconnaissance regiment, and the Hong Kong Government Air Services, used for search and rescue duties.

Nationality and Emigration

Under the British Nationality Act 1981, some 3·3 million Hong Kong residents became British Dependent Territories citizens

(BDTCs), the remainder of the population holding Hong Kong resident permits giving no form of citizenship under British law. The Hong Kong (British Nationality) Order 1986 enables BDTCs in Hong Kong to acquire a new form of British nationality—called British National (Overseas)—and to retain this status for the rest of their lives; if they do not acquire this status by 1 July 1997, and would otherwise be stateless, they automatically become British Overseas citizens.

Hong Kong has had a highly mobile population, many people having migrated from China and elsewhere. There is also a well-established tradition of going overseas for education, training, career development and permanent settlement. In the years from 1980 to 1986, the average yearly outflow was about 20,000. However, in 1987 the numbers rose to 30,000, were 45,800 in 1988 and by 1990 had reached 62,000. Although several thousand former Hong Kong residents return to the territory each year, often having acquired foreign nationality, this exodus of talent poses a threat to the competitiveness of the economy, the efficiency of the public service and the effectiveness of the education system.

Many are leaving Hong Kong only to obtain the insurance of a foreign passport and would prefer to stay if they could acquire such an assurance without leaving. The British Government wishes to preserve the territory's stability and prosperity, an objective mentioned in the Joint Declaration. With these considerations in mind the Government proposed in December 1989 that British citizenship should be given to 50,000 key people, their spouses and dependent children under 18, without their having to leave Hong Kong in order to qualify. Legislation giving effect to these proposals was passed by the

British Parliament in 1990 and the scheme was launched on 1 December 1990.

Of the 50,000 places, 36,200 are being allocated according to a points system to people with a key role in maintaining prosperity and successful administration. Seven thousand places are being given to members of the disciplined services such as the police and the fire service; 6,300 places to people who may be vulnerable after 1997 by reason of their service in the interests of the Crown, or other sensitive activities; and 500 places to major entrepreneurs.

Vietnamese Boat People

Since 1975 more than 178,000 Vietnamese boat people have arrived in Hong Kong, which has continued to operate a policy of first asylum. Before 1988 Hong Kong treated all arrivals as refugees for resettlement in the West. Britain accepted over 13,000.

From the early 1980s it became increasingly obvious that the majority of those leaving Vietnam were economic migrants rather than people fleeing persecution and that the United States and other Western countries would not accept these people for resettlement as refugees. The situation in Hong Kong became serious in the mid-1980s, when the number of new arrivals began to exceed the rate of resettlement. A major new influx in 1987 and 1988 led to the introduction of screening in Hong Kong in June 1988.

A second international conference held in Geneva in June 1989 endorsed a comprehensive plan of action providing for the maintenance of first asylum, the introduction of screening of new arrivals on a region-wide basis, the resettlement of those found to be refugees after screening and the repatriation of those found not to be refugees. Screening in Hong Kong has been developed with the full co-operation of the United Nations High Commissioner for Refugees (UNHCR). The criterion used is that contained in a 1951 United Nations Convention and the 1967 protocol relating to the status of refugees. The Convention states that a person is a refugee if he or she has a well founded fear of being persecuted for reasons of race, religion, nationality, membership of a particular social group or political opinion and who, because of this fear, is unwilling to avail himself or herself of the protection of his or her country of nationality.

In April 1991 Vietnam reaffirmed its undertaking that no one returned to Vietnam would be persecuted and that the UNHCR would have unhindered access to those who returned. More than 20,000 asylum seekers in Hong Kong have taken advantage of this voluntary repatriation programme. Britain has pledged £3 million to help non-refugees returning to Vietnam to be reintegrated into their community.

Since 29 October 1991 there have been three flights returning non-refugees under an Orderly Repatriation Programme. Now that the British and Hong Kong authorities have demonstrated that they have the will and the means to return non-refugees, the number of Vietnamese arriving in Hong Kong has dropped dramatically and record numbers are volunteering to return under UNHCR auspices.

The Economy

Hong Kong is one of the world's largest trading economies, has the world's biggest container port and is a major financial centre, with substantial international investment. Its principal natural asset is its sheltered harbour, the only developed deep-water port on the Chinese coast.

Hong Kong's development into a commercial centre began in the 1840s. It was located on the trade routes of the Far East and it became the hub of a burgeoning entrepôt trade with China. Trade and commerce were the main economic activities for more than a century.

After 1945 the territory had to develop new sources of income to support its greatly increased population (see p. 14). Hong Kong turned to manufacturing, starting with textiles and clothing but diversifying later into many other products, including plastics, electrical and electronic goods, scientific instruments, watches and photographic and optical equipment. The traditional entrepôt trade with China and the rest of East Asia has revived in recent years. Service industries have expanded rapidly because of growing domestic incomes and Hong Kong's development as an important international financial and tourist centre.

Government intervention is kept to a minimum, except where social considerations are regarded as overriding, for example, the provision of public housing. Tax rates are relatively low. There are no tariffs or other restrictions on external trade. The link between the Hong Kong and United States dollars—established in 1983 at the fixed rate of HK$7·8 to US$1—has helped to provide a framework of stability and certainty which has benefited external trade.

Unemployment is very low, the seasonally adjusted rate averaging only 1·8 per cent in the fourth quarter of 1991.

Economic Growth

Following the signature of the Joint Declaration, Hong Kong enjoyed rapid economic growth. In 1986 and 1987 real growth was 11 per cent and 14 per cent respectively. The pace of growth in real terms of gross domestic product, however, fell to 7 per cent in 1988 and 2·8 per cent in 1989. Overall growth in gross domestic product was 3 per cent in 1990. This was mainly attributable to more moderate overseas demand for Hong Kong products and constraints on the supply side following rapid growth in the period between 1986 and 1988.

Structure and Development

Hong Kong depends on imports for virtually all its requirements, including food, raw materials, fuel and water. It has, therefore, had to export to generate the foreign exchange earnings to pay for the imports and to sustain a rising standard of living for the population. Between 1981 and 1991 Hong Kong's domestic exports grew at an average rate of about 7 per cent in real terms, roughly twice the growth rate of world trade. In 1990 and 1991 domestic exports showed no change in real terms.

The biggest contributions to gross domestic product are made by services (69 per cent in 1990) and manufacturing (17 per cent). The share of services in total employment rose from 41 per cent in 1971 to 63 per cent in 1991; manufacturing took up 28 per cent of employment in 1991 compared with 47 per cent in 1971.

Services

Rapid growth in external trade over the past decades enabled services to flourish and diversify. There was a rapid increase in finance and business services, including banking, insurance, real estate and a wide range of other professional services. In addition, a large network of supermarkets, department stores and modern shopping centres has developed to meet the needs of a more affluent population. Restaurants and hotels have experienced a substantial rise in business, reinforced by the rapid growth of tourism. In September 1991 some 1,560,000 were employed in services.

In 1991 more than 6 million visitors came to Hong Kong, earnings from tourism reaching HK$40,000 million. Taiwan and Japan accounted for 21·5 per cent and 20·9 per cent respectively. Others came from South East Asia (16·8 per cent), and South Korea (3·1 per cent). Some 30·7 per cent of visitors came from the United States, Canada, Western Europe, Australia and New Zealand.

There has been a growth in the convention and exhibition business from 15 international events in 1976 to 500 in 1991. A new convention and exhibition centre—the largest in Asia—was officially opened by the Prince of Wales in November 1989.

Manufacturing

About 90 per cent of manufacturing output is exported. Because of the limited amount of usable land, the industry concentrates on the production of light manufactures. The majority of factories are accommodated in high rise multi-storey industrial buildings. The many small firms supporting an extensive local sub-contracting system have greatly facilitated the shifts in production necessary to cope with frequent changes in demand patterns. Increasing use has also been made of outward processing facilities in China for handling some of the production processes.

The share of the textile industry in the net output of manufacturing declined from 27 per cent in 1973 to 16 per cent in 1989 and its share in manufacturing employment from 21 per cent to 15 per cent. Offsetting this decline was the expansion of the clothing, electrical appliances and electronics, and watches and clocks industries; between 1973 and 1989, their shares in net output rose from 30 per cent to 40 per cent and their shares in manufacturing employment from 38 per cent to 45 per cent. In 1991, 654,662 people were employed in manufacturing. The largest categories were clothing (223,840 employees); electronics (71,466); textiles (62,438); plastics (42,522); and watches and clocks (23,935).

The Hong Kong Government's industrial policies aim at maintaining an infrastructure which enables manufacturing businesses to function efficiently and at providing services designed to enable industry to become more competitive. It encourages technology transfer through an inward investment programme. In 1991 it approved the establishment of a technology centre to encourage the growth of technology-based firms; the centre will become fully operational by 1993.

Trade

In 1991 the largest markets for domestic exports were the United States (27 per cent), China (24 per cent), Germany (8 per cent) and Britain (6 per cent). Other important markets were Taiwan, Canada, the Netherlands and France.

Clothing was responsible for 33 per cent of exports by value, followed by miscellaneous manufactured articles (11 per cent) and electrical machinery, apparatus and appliances (8 per cent). Textiles contributed another 8 per cent to the total. Other important exports included telecommunications and sound recording and reproducing equipment (7 per cent), as well as office machines and automatic data-processing equipment (8 per cent).

Imports of raw materials and semi-manufactured goods represented 38 per cent of total imports. Another 39 per cent of imports consisted of consumer goods. Capital goods accounted for 15 per cent of imports and foodstuffs 5 per cent. The remainder consisted of mineral fuels, lubricants and related materials. China provided 38 per cent of imports and Japan 16 per cent. About a third of food imports are supplied by China.

Hong Kong possesses autonomy in the conduct of its external commercial relations. The Governor has executive authority to conclude and implement trade agreements with states, regions and international organisations and to conduct all other aspects of external commercial relations. The Hong Kong Government pursues a free trade policy and is a contracting party to the GATT (see p. 9).

Agriculture and Fisheries

Only about 8 per cent of the land area is usable for agriculture because the territory consists largely of steep unproductive mountain land.

Agriculture is directed towards the production of high quality fresh foods through intensive land use. Local farmers produce about 28 per cent of fresh vegetables, 32 per cent of live poultry, 10 per cent of live pigs and 13 per cent of freshwater fish consumed. The fishing fleet of some 4,500 vessels supplies about 70 per cent of all live and fresh marine fish eaten.

The Agriculture and Fisheries Department provides technical support services for local farmers and fishermen.

Economic Relations with China

Since the adoption of open-door economic policies by China in the late 1970s, the economic relationship between Hong Kong and China has developed at a rapid pace. Hong Kong and China are each other's largest trading partner. China accounts for 24 per cent of Hong Kong domestic exports and 38 per cent of its imports. In addition, more than 28 per cent of goods re-exported through Hong Kong are destined for China.

Hong Kong provides two-thirds of total external investment in China. In Guangdong Province alone about 3 million people are working for Hong Kong companies through joint ventures or in work commissioned by them.

Chinese investment in Hong Kong has increased and has diversified into banking, telecommunications, property development, financial services, warehousing, manufacturing and infrastructural projects.

Economic Relations with Britain

Britain's visible exports to Hong Kong were worth nearly £1,390 million in 1991; imports from Hong Kong were worth nearly £2,200 million.

The British Trade Commission in Hong Kong provides commercial services for British exporters and businessmen and for

Hong Kong importers seeking sources of supply. The Commission is an overseas post of the Foreign and Commonwealth Office (FCO) and works closely with the Department of Trade and Industry. The Information Section also presents British Government policy generally and deals with press enquiries. When British sovereignty ceases in 1997, the Commission will be replaced by a Consulate General.

Financial Services

Hong Kong has developed into an important international financial centre because of its close economic links with China and other economies in South-East Asia, as well as its excellent communications with the rest of the world. Its favourable geographical position also means that business can be done in Hong Kong when London and New York financial institutions are closed. Most of the world's top banks operate in Hong Kong and have 152 offices there.

At the end of 1991 there were 163 licensed banks which operate current or savings accounts. Deposit taking companies— 159 at the end of 1991—are registered with the Commissioner of Banking. In addition, there were 240 authorised insurance companies of which 129 were from overseas. Also from overseas were 143 of the 279 registered securities dealers and 36 of the 96 commodities dealers.

Regulation of the Financial Sector

Following the world stock market crash in October 1987, which severely affected the Hong Kong market, the Stock and Futures Exchanges underwent substantial changes in their constitution and management to remedy weaknesses revealed during the market collapse. Established in May 1989, the statutory Securities and Futures Commission supervises the operations of the securities, financial investment and commodities futures industry. The

Governor appoints the directors and may give policy directions to the Commission.

Laws require the registration of dealers, dealing partnerships, investment advisers and other intermediaries. There are powers to investigate suspected malpractice and a compensation fund is maintained to compensate clients of defaulting brokers. It is an offence to use fraudulent means to induce investors to buy or sell securities.

Steps have been taken to tackle the problem of insider dealing in shares. In 1990 the Legislative Council passed a law requiring substantial shareholders, directors and chief executives of listed companies incorporated in Hong Kong to disclose their shareholdings and share dealings. This is designed to make insider dealing harder to conceal and provides for much stiffer penalties for those found guilty. The legislation came into force on 1 September 1991.

Monetary Policy

Unlike most major economies, Hong Kong has no central bank. The Monetary Affairs Branch of the Government Secretariat performs most central bank functions, including prudential supervision of financial institutions, managing official foreign exchange reserves and backing the note issue.

Dollar notes are issued by two commercial banks—the Hong Kong and Shanghai Bank, which also manages the clearing system, and the Standard Chartered Bank. The two banks issue notes against holdings of certificates of indebtedness issued and redeemed by the Hong Kong Government Exchange Fund against payments in US dollars at the fixed rate of HK$7·80 to US$1. The Exchange Fund also holds the backing to the note issue and the bulk of the Hong Kong Government's financial assets. The Fund intervenes where necessary in the local money market or foreign currency markets to maintain stability. It is managed by the Office of the Exchange Fund which was set up within the Monetary Affairs Branch in February 1991. The Office is responsible for monetary policy and oversees the operations of the money and foreign exchange markets. It also manages the assets of the Exchange Fund.

Transport and Utilities

Transport

The objectives of Hong Kong's transport policy are to maintain the mobility of passengers and freight in order to support economic growth and to meet the social, commercial and recreational needs of the community. Efforts are made to restrain private car use by developing high quality public transport.

Civil Aviation

Hong Kong's international airport is situated at Kai Tak and handled 19·2 million passengers in 1991, as well as 852,000 tonnes of cargo. About 18 per cent of the territory's imports arrive by air while exports by air are about 30 per cent of the total.

Because the airport is now reaching saturation point, the Governor announced plans in October 1989 to build a new international airport at Chek Lap Kok to the north of Lantau Island as a replacement. It is scheduled to come into operation in 1997. Initially it will have one runway and will be able to operate 24 hours a day with a capacity of 35 million passengers a year and 1·5 million tonnes of cargo. Supporting infrastructure will include extensive road and rail links, including a major suspension bridge and a new town. The new airport will be located on a 1,250-hectare area off the northern shore of Lantau and will be formed primarily by levelling the islands of Chep Lap Kok and Lam Chau and by using the excavated materials and marine sand fill for reclamation.

Building the new airport and the associated rail and road links will be the largest project ever undertaken in Hong Kong and one of the largest of its kind in the world. Many international companies will be involved in the funding, design and implementation of the project.

In September 1991 the British and Chinese Governments signed a memorandum of understanding on the construction of the new airport. This means that the project is going ahead.

Hong Kong has three airlines, of which the largest is Cathay Pacific Airways. In 1990 the number of scheduled airlines serving the territory was 46, connecting it with 80 cities throughout the world.

In accordance with the provisions of the Joint Declaration, Hong Kong's air service agreements are gradually being separated from those of Britain.

The Port

Hong Kong's port is one of the busiest in the world. It handled 104 million tonnes of cargo in 1991. The Kwai Chung container port has 12 berths with more than 4,000 metres of quay. In view of the growth in traffic, a four-berth terminal is being built at Stonecutters Island, opposite Kwai Chung. Another terminal is to be built on nearby Tsing Yi Island. Plans have been drawn up to develop five container terminals on the Tsing Chau peninsula on Lantau between 1997 and 2011.

A Port Development Board is responsible for organising the necessary consultation on future port planning, including land, marine and transport aspects.

The port has extensive facilities for ship repairing and dry-docking; vessels of up to 150,000 deadweight tonnes can be accommodated.

Ships registered in Hong Kong follow similar standards of construction, safety and manning to those registered in Britain. Hitherto this has been accomplished by the extension of United Kingdom legislation to Hong Kong. The Sino-British Joint Declaration made provision for a shipping register under Hong Kong legislation. In December 1990 the new Hong Kong Shipping Register was created and reflects the Government's commitment to the highest standards of maritime safety.

Roads

The territory has one of the highest vehicle densities in the world; at the end of 1991 there were nearly 380,000 licensed vehicles and about 1,530 kilometres of roads. There were over 212,000 registered private cars and about 134,000 registered goods vehicles. There are two road tunnels linking Hong Kong Island and Kowloon. The airport tunnel provides direct road access from the central area of Kowloon to the international airport. The north and south sides of Hong Kong Island are linked by the Aberdeen tunnel. Kowloon is linked by road tunnel to Sha Tin and the north-eastern New Territories. Other road tunnels link Sha Tin and Tsuen Wan and Kwun Tong to Tseung Wan O New Town. Major investment in roads continues to be made by the Hong Kong Government.

There are three road crossings with China at Lok Ma Chau, Man Kam To and Sha Tau Kok. Goods vehicles account for 95 per cent of road traffic with China, reflecting the rapid growth in trade and industrial links; in 1991 average daily vehicle traffic movements across the border were 15,900.

Railways and Buses
The five rail systems include a well-used underground rapid transit metro, a busy suburban railway, a new light railway, an electric tramway on Hong Kong Island and a renovated funicular railway.

The Mass Transit Railway, with 38 stations and 43 kilometres (26 miles) of route, has three lines which carry 2·3 million passengers a day. The system links Hong Kong Island with Tsuen Wan and Kwun Tong.

The Kowloon–Canton Railway running from the Kowloon Peninsula to Lo Wu at the border with China was double tracked and electrified in the early 1980s; under the control of the Kowloon–Canton Railway Corporation, the 34-km (21-mile) railway provides a suburban service to the new towns of the north-eastern New Territories, which carries 537,000 passengers a day. There are freight services to and from China and four daily passenger services each way between Kowloon and Guangzhou.

The Corporation also owns and operates the new 28-km (17·3-mile) light railway in the north-western New Territories, which opened in 1988. The system is being extended to 30·4 km. By the end of 1991 some 268,000 boardings a day were handled by the railway.

Three franchised bus companies carry 3·4 million passengers a day on a network of 412 regular routes. Many bus routes interchange with the various rail systems. In addition, there are nearly 6,900 minibuses.

Ferries

The majority of ferry services are provided by two licensed operators. Eight minor ferry services were operated by six licensed operators.

Electricity, Gas and Water

Electricity is supplied by two privately owned companies whose operation is monitored by the Hong Kong Government. The Castle Peak Station complex is one of the largest in the world. Hong Kong plans to purchase up to 70 per cent of the electricity generated from the nuclear power station in Guangdong Province being built by a Chinese/Hong Kong joint venture company; the station, situated at Naya Bay, will comprise two 900-MW pressurised water reactors scheduled for commissioning in 1992 and 1993.

Town gas is supplied for domestic, commercial and industrial use by the Hong Kong and China Gas Company. It is distributed to its customers for cooking and heating purposes. Liquefied petroleum gas is supplied by oil companies and imported by sea; about 64 per cent of sales is distributed in portable cylinders and the remainder through piped gas systems. The 1990 Gas Safety Ordinance and its associated regulations cover all aspects of fuel gas importation, manufacture, storage, transport, supply and use.

Water from China is the major single source of supply, amounting to over 570 million cubic metres; this will rise to 660 million cubic metres in 1994–99. All future increases in demand will be met from this source. In December 1989 agreement was reached with China to increase the water supply to a maximum of 1,100 million cubic metres per year beyond 1994.

Telecommunications

With around 60 telephones for every 100 people, Hong Kong has one of the highest telephone densities in Asia. By the end of 1991 there were an estimated 3·4 million telephones served by 2·6 million exchange lines.

International direct dialling is available to more than 208 overseas countries and territories, including over 650 destinations in China.

Public telecommunications services are provided under franchise by the Hong Kong Telephone Company Limited and Hong Kong Telecom International Limited. The former has the exclusive right to provide the public telephone service until 30 June 1995, and the latter is responsible until September 2006 for international services including telephone, telex, telegram, facsimile and data transmission facilities.

Services outside the scope of the two franchises, such as mobile telephones and radio paging, are provided on a competitive basis.

Hong Kong is linked to other territories by overland and submarine cables, satellites and terrestrial radio links. A submarine cable links Hong Kong with Singapore and Taiwan. There is also a Hong Kong–Guangzhou optical fibre cable. A regional telecommunications satellite has been successfully launched by a Hong Kong company in a rocket from China; it provides telecommunications services covering an area from the Middle East to Japan, including Hong Kong and China.

The Postmaster General administers legislation governing the establishment and operation of all telecommunications services and advises the Hong Kong Government.

Aerial view of Sha Tin, one of Hong Kong's largest new towns.

New housing estate with garden, Kowloon.

Exchange Square, home of Hong Kong's Stock Exchange.

Interior of Hong Kong Stock Exchange.

A meeting of the Hong Kong Legislative Council.

Po Lin Monastery, Lantau Island.

Hong Kong's new Cultural Centre.

Social Programmes

Although Hong Kong does not have a western-style welfare state, considerable resources are concentrated on the vulnerable sections of the population and on young people. Public housing, the health service and education are all subsidised from public funds.

Education

Hong Kong's prosperity over the past 20 years has increased the demand for better education. The Hong Kong Government's objectives are to improve the quality of education and to ensure that it is consistent with the changing requirements of the economy.

Schools

In September 1991 nearly 194,000 children aged between three and five attended some 767 privately operated kindergartens; there is a fee remission scheme for needy parents.

Free primary education for pupils aged between six and twelve is available in all government schools and in nearly all grant-aided schools. In September 1991, primary school enrolment totalled nearly 516,000. Most children attend primary school either in the morning or in the afternoon. The Hong Kong Government's long-term aim is to work towards whole-day schooling for all primary classes.

Education in junior secondary schools is free. For senior secondary education, the policy is to provide by 1992 subsidised places for about 85 per cent of the 15-year-old population. Places for a further 10 per cent of the age group will be provided on full-time craft courses of vocational training.

In 1991 a direct subsidy system for private schools was introduced in order to improve the quality and diversity of education. Under the scheme, any secondary school which is not run by the Government and which meets specified standards receives a public subsidy for each student enrolled. Such schools are free to set their own curriculum, entrance requirements and fee levels, with minimum government control.

There are three types of secondary school—grammar, technical and pre-vocational. In 1991 there were 397 grammar schools with a total enrolment of over 395,000. These schools offer a five-year secondary course in academic, cultural and practical subjects leading to the Hong Kong Certificate of Education Examination; in addition, most offer a two-year sixth-form course leading to the Hong Kong Advanced Level Examination.

There are 22 technical schools and 23 pre-vocational schools providing technical and practical courses for nearly 41,000 pupils.

Sixty-two special schools are available for blind, deaf, physically handicapped and mentally handicapped children and for those with learning difficulties. Children identified as having special educational needs are as far as possible integrated into ordinary schools. They are only placed in special schools when they cannot benefit from the ordinary school programme.

Tertiary and Vocational Education
Under current government plans, some 25 per cent of young people in the relevant age groups will be able to take degree courses in universities and other institutions by 1994–95.

There are three universities—the University of Hong Kong (9,888 students), situated on Hong Kong Island; the Chinese University of Hong Kong (10,249 students) near Sha Tin in the New Territories; and the Hong Kong University of Science and Technology, which opened in October 1991 with 831 students.

The Hong Kong Polytechnic offers courses to meet the demands of commerce, industry and the community. In October 1991 some 10,935 students were enrolled on full-time and sandwich courses and 16,005 on part-time courses. The other polytechnic is the City Polytechnic of Hong Kong which has 7,040 full-time, 5,540 part-time and 336 sandwich course students. Another degree-awarding institution is the Hong Kong Baptist College which is fully funded by the Government; it has 3,490 full-time and 1,294 part-time students.

The University and Polytechnic Grants Committee advises the Hong Kong Government on funding requirements for higher education and administers government grants for universities and polytechnics.

The Hong Kong Council for Academic Accreditation was set up to ensure that the standards of degrees awarded by non-university institutions are comparable to those of internationally recognised degrees.

The Open Learning Institute of Hong Kong was established as a degree-awarding institution in 1989 to provide a second chance for those who were unable to go on to further education after leaving school. There is a multimedia approach to instruction, including programmes on television, printed texts and audio-visual material, and extensive tutorial support. By April 1991, about 16,500 students were pursuing their studies in this way.

Industrial training is promoted and co-ordinated by the Vocational Training Council, which operates training centres providing places for over 30,000 trainees on a full- or part-time basis. The Council also has eight technical institutes providing technician level courses for just over 57,500 full- or part-time students.

Four colleges of education train non-graduate teachers for primary and secondary schools. In October 1991 there were 2,452 full-time students and a similar number taking in-service training and retraining courses.

Health Services

The population's general level of health remains good. Infant mortality has remained below seven per 1,000 live births and average life expectancy is 80 for females and 75 for males.

The health service is subsidised. In 1991 more than 646,000 patients were treated at the 35 public hospitals. A major hospital building programme is under way. In 1990 a new 1,600-bed hospital in Tuen Man was opened and a major extension to the Queen Mary hospital has been completed. The new 1,600-bed Pamela Youde Hospital in Chai Wan is scheduled for completion in 1992. Public hospitals are managed and controlled by an independent statutory Hospital Authority.

The Hong Kong Government operates 66 general out-patient clinics as well as the mobile dispensaries and floating clinics which take medical services to the outlying islands and the more remote areas of the New Territories. There is also a flying doctor service for inaccessible areas.

The Government also has 45 maternal and child health centres providing comprehensive care for women of child-bearing age and children aged up to five years. Ante-natal and post-natal medical consultation as well as family planning services are offered to women. Immunisation programmes are carried out against tuberculosis, diphtheria, whooping cough, tetanus, poliomyelitis, measles, mumps, rubella and viral hepatitis B. About 90 per cent of new-born babies attend the centres.

The Government-funded Family Planning Association of Hong Kong runs 26 birth control clinics.

There is a school dental care service providing regular examinations, treatment and oral health education for primary school children. An independent board operates the school medical service scheme which operates on a voluntary basis; a small fee is charged for each inspection and the Government makes a contribution for each pupil enrolled and pays the costs of administration.

Basic medical training is provided by the medical schools of the University of Hong Kong and the Chinese University of Hong Kong. Graduates are awarded degrees recognised by the General Medical Council of Great Britain. The Hong Kong Government is establishing a statutory academy of medicine to organise and supervise postgraduate and continuing medical education.

The Hong Kong Polytechnic trains radiographers, physiotherapists, medical laboratory technicians and dental technicians.

Basic training for general nurses is conducted at government, government-assisted and private hospitals. There are nine schools for training students to be registered nurses and 11 for training pupils to be enrolled nurses. The training of psychiatric nurses takes place at two hospitals; three new training schools for psychiatric nurses are planned for the next decade.

Drug Abuse

Drug abuse, particularly heroin addiction, is a long-standing problem. The exact number of addicts is not known but is thought to be about 41,000.

The Hong Kong Government has a comprehensive anti-drug abuse programme consisting of law enforcement, treatment and rehabilitation, preventive education and publicity, and international co-operation. Courts are empowered to confiscate drug traffickers' assets, and legislation counters the illegal laundering of money derived from drug trafficking. Joint anti-drug operations take place with overseas law enforcement agencies.

The Department of Health operates 25 methadone treatment clinics for out-patients designed to reduce or eliminate an addict's reliance on heroin or other opiates. A large voluntary in-patient treatment programme is run by the Society for the Aid and Rehabilitation of Drug Abusers. A compulsory drug treatment programme is operated by the Correctional Services Department.

The Hong Kong Government devotes considerable resources to anti-drugs publicity campaigns in schools.

Hong Kong plays an active part in international anti-drug operations by maintaining close links with the United Nations, intergovernmental agencies such as Interpol and the Customs Co-operation Council, and governments in South-East Asia, Europe and North America.

Social Welfare

There is a non-contributory social security system designed to meet the needs of vulnerable groups requiring financial assistance. The means-tested public assistance scheme raises the income of needy individuals and families to a level where essential requirements are met. Additional allowances are paid to disabled and elderly people to cover their special needs. The minimum qualifying age for an old-age allowance was lowered to 65 in 1991.

Direct welfare services are also financed by the Hong Kong Government, the majority operated by voluntary welfare agencies through a system of subsidies. Services range from day creches for very young children to residential homes for elderly people; family and child care services are designed to strengthen the family as a unit by helping families to solve their problems or avoid them altogether.

Facilities for disabled people include counselling services, day and residential centres, special schools, workshops, work activity centres, and recreational and transport arrangements. Allowances are paid to severely disabled people, regardless of age and financial means.

Training of professional social workers is provided by the universities, polytechnics and post-secondary colleges.

Housing

Over 3 million people live in public housing—86 per cent of them in rented flats and the rest in their own homes. The Hong Kong Housing Authority is responsible for co-ordinating public housing programmes. It advises the Governor and plans, builds and manages public housing estates. Over 40,000 flats were produced by the Authority in 1991. It owns and manages some 645,000 rental flats in 146 housing estates.

The Housing Authority is responsible for the Home Ownership Scheme, which assists lower/middle-income families and public housing tenants to become home owners by providing flats for sale at prices below market value. Also operated by the

Authority is the Home Purchase Loan Scheme, which assists people to buy flats in the private sector.

There are still about 290,000 people living in squatter settlements. Steps have been taken by the Housing Authority to provide basic services and safety facilities in needy squatter areas not yet scheduled for clearance. By the mid-1990s, all clearance should be completed.

The Hong Kong Government provides capital assistance and other funds plus land for the Authority, which is responsible for its own finance and management. Many members of the Authority and its committees also serve the community as Legislative, Urban or Regional councillors or as members of district boards or area committees.

Because of the acute land shortage, blocks of up to 36 storeys are built. In terms of open space, landscaping, recreational facilities and flat layout, modern public sector estates are well up to the standard of good private developments. Standard facilities in new developments include a shopping centre, restaurants, clinics, car parks, gardens and play areas, kindergartens, schools and a hostel for elderly people.

The Housing Authority is also redeveloping older estates whose facilities are not up to present standards.

On average, Housing Authority tenants pay 7 per cent of their income in rent which is reviewed every two years. Rent levels are about one-third to one-quarter of current market rents.

The Environment

Hong Kong has inevitably suffered the environmental consequences of industrial development and economic growth. In June 1989 the Hong Kong Government published a White Paper on pollution setting out the main problems and outlining a comprehensive plan for tackling them over the next decade. The main problems concern the discharge of sewage and industrial effluent into coastal waters; the pollution of streams in the New Territories by livestock wastes, smoke and other emissions from diesel-engined vehicles, power stations and factories using high sulphur fuel; and noise pollution from construction activities and high density traffic.

Environmental factors are considered during the planning and assessment of major developments, for example, the choice of Chek Lap Kok as the site for the new airport.

Different parts of Hong Kong waters are progressively being designated as water control zones. Industrial and commercial polluters can be prosecuted if they discharge pollutants in these areas. Standards have been drawn up setting out the minimum acceptable quality for effluent discharged to sewers, drains, inland waters and coastal waters. A programme is being implemented to upgrade the sewerage system.

Three large landfills are being developed in remote parts of the New Territories to which waste will be delivered from the urban areas, allowing urban incinerators and landfills close to urban areas to be phased out.

A chemical waste treatment centre is being developed to help put a stop to indiscriminate disposal of such waste. Under regulations recently enacted, all chemical wastes have to be treated and disposed of at licensed facilities; collection and transport of such waste is carried out by licensed collectors.

In order to combat air pollution, the whole of Hong Kong has been declared an air control zone. The Government can issue notices requiring the abatement of air pollution and the modification or repair of chimneys. Legislation also requires certain specified processes to obtain a licence. Regulations also limit the sulphur content of liquid fuel to 0·5 per cent by weight, the result being a dramatic drop in sulphur dioxide levels. Measures being taken against pollution from motor vehicle emissions include the introduction of unleaded petrol at all filling stations from April 1991 and a requirement that all light duty vehicles and passenger cars registered after the start of 1992 should comply with new stringent emission standards.

As part of Hong Kong's contribution towards protection of the ozone layer, legislation has been passed prohibiting local manufacture of chlorofluorocarbons (CFCs) and halons; this also imposes controls on the import and export of these substances.

The Media and the Arts

There is freedom of expression in Hong Kong's vigorous information media. With nearly 70 daily newspapers and around 600 periodicals, the territory has one of the highest newspaper readerships in Asia. One of the English language dailies publishes a daily braille edition. It is also the South East Asian base for many international newspapers, magazines and news agencies. Agencies represented include Associated Press, Reuters, United Press International, Agence France-Presse and Kyodo News Service of Japan. *Newsweek* and *Time* magazines have Hong Kong printed editions. Hong Kong is also the base for the regional magazines *Asiaweek* and the *Far Eastern Economic Review*, as well as the *Asian Wall Street Journal* and an edition of the *International Herald Tribune*.

More than 98 per cent of households own one television set or more and 67 per cent a video cassette recorder. There are two private television companies, each of which provide one Chinese and one English-language service. The two companies together transmit an average of over 550 hours of programmes per week.

Radio Television Hong Kong (RTHK) is a publicly financed radio and television station which produces 12 hours of public affairs television programmes a week for transmission by the two commercial stations. It also produces educational programmes for the Government's Education Television Service which uses the transmission facilities of the commercial stations for eight hours every week day during term time.

In 1991 the first Hong Kong-based satellite television operator started broadcasting; it has five channels and is also licensed to transmit BBC World Service radio programmes throughout Asia.

Seven of the 15 radio channels are operated by RTHK (Radio), six by two commercial stations and two by the British Forces Broadcasting Service. As a publicly funded station RTHK is charged with providing balanced and objective broadcasting services to inform, educate and entertain. Its news and public affairs programmes aim to provide fast, accurate and in-depth news reports. Its main Chinese and English services operate 24 hours a day.

Cinema-going is a popular leisure activity. Although imported films continue to be popular, there is also a flourishing local film industry. In 1991 locally produced films totalled 211.

Hong Kong has two professional orchestras (including a Chinese music orchestra), three full-time dance companies, three professional drama groups and hundreds of amateur groups, including choirs, folk dance groups and drama clubs. The Council for the Performing Arts advises the Government on the development of the performing arts and disburses funds on performing arts activities. The Hong Kong Academy for Performing Arts provides training, education and research in the performing and related technical arts.

The Urban and Regional Councils present year-round programmes of music, opera, dance, films and entertainment. There is also an annual arts festival.

In 1989 the Hong Kong Cultural Centre was opened as the main cultural venue in the territory. It has a concert hall, a theatre and a studio theatre. The Hong Kong Museum of Art is accommodated in a new building at the Cultural centre. In 1991 the four-storey Hong Kong Science Museum was opened. There is also a Hong Kong Museum of History and a railway museum.

Appendix:

JOINT DECLARATION OF
THE GOVERNMENT OF THE UNITED KINGDOM
OF GREAT BRITAIN AND NORTHERN IRELAND
AND
THE GOVERNMENT OF THE PEOPLE'S REPUBLIC
OF CHINA ON THE QUESTION OF HONG KONG

The Government of the United Kingdom of Great Britain and Northern Ireland and the Government of the People's Republic of China have reviewed with satisfaction the friendly relations existing between the two Governments and peoples in recent years and agreed that a proper negotiated settlement of the question of Hong Kong, which is left over from the past, is conducive to the maintenance of the prosperity and stability of Hong Kong and to the further strengthening and development of the relations between the two countries on a new basis. To this end, they have, after talks between the delegations of the two Governments, agreed to declare as follows:

1. The Government of the People's Republic of China declares that to recover the Hong Kong area (including Hong Kong Island, Kowloon and the New Territories, hereinafter referred to as Hong Kong) is the common aspiration of the entire Chinese people, and that it has decided to resume the exercise of sovereignty over Hong Kong with effect from 1 July 1997.

2. The Government of the United Kingdom declares that it will restore Hong Kong to the People's Republic of China with effect from 1 July 1997.

3. The Government of the People's Republic of China declares that the basic policies of the People's Republic of China regarding Hong Kong are as follows:

(1)   Upholding national unity and territorial integrity and taking account of the history of Hong Kong and its realities, the People's Republic of China has decided to establish, in accordance with the provisions of Article 31 of the Constitution of the People's Republic of China, a Hong Kong Special Administrative Region upon resuming the exercise of sovereignty over Hong Kong.

(2)   The Hong Kong Special Administrative Region will be directly under the authority of the Central People's Government of the People's Republic of China. The Hong Kong Special Administrative Region will enjoy a high degree of autonomy, except in foreign and defence affairs which are the responsibilities of the Central People's Government.

(3)   The Hong Kong Special Administrative Region will be vested with executive, legislative, and independent judicial power, including that of final adjudication. The laws currently in force in Hong Kong will remain basically unchanged.

(4)   The Government of the Hong Kong Special Administrative Region will be composed of local inhabitants. The chief executive will be appointed by the Central People's Government on the basis of the results of elections or consultations to be held locally. Principal officials will be nominated by the chief executive of the Hong Kong Special Administrative Region for appointment by the Central People's Government. Chinese and foreign nationals previously working in the public and police services in the government departments of Hong Kong may remain in employment. British and other foreign nationals may also be employed to serve as advisers or hold certain public posts in government departments of the Hong Kong Special Administrative Region.

(5) The current social and economic systems in Hong Kong will remain unchanged, and so will the life-style. Rights and freedoms, including those of the person, of speech, of the press, of assembly, of association, of travel, of movement, of correspondence, of strike, of choice of occupation, of academic research and of religious belief will be ensured by law in the Hong Kong Special Administrative Region. Private property, ownership of enterprises, legitimate right of inheritance and foreign investment will be protected by law.

(6) The Hong Kong Special Administrative Region will retain the status of a free port and a separate customs territory.

(7) The Hong Kong Special Administrative Region will retain the status of an international financial centre, and its markets for foreign exchange, gold, securities and futures will continue. There will be free flow of capital. The Hong Kong dollar will continue to circulate and remain freely convertible.

(8) The Hong Kong Special Administrative Region will have independent finances. The Central People's Government will not levy taxes on the Hong Kong Special Administrative Region.

(9) The Hong Kong Special Administrative Region may establish mutually beneficial economic relations with the United Kingdom and other countries, whose economic interests in Hong Kong will be given due regard.

(10) Using the name of 'Hong Kong, China', the Hong Kong Special Administrative Region may on its own maintain and develop economic and cultural relations and conclude relevant agreements with states, regions and relevant international organisations.

The Government of the Hong Kong Special Administrative Region may on its own issue travel documents for entry into and exit from Hong Kong.

(11) The maintenance of public order in the Hong Kong Special Administrative Region will be the responsibility of the Government of the Hong Kong Special Administrative Region.

(12)   The above-stated basic policies of the People's Republic of China regarding Hong Kong and the elaboration of them in Annex I to this Joint Declaration will be stipulated, in a Basic Law of the Hong Kong Special Administrative Region of the People's Republic of China, by the National People's Congress of the People's Republic of China, and they will remain unchanged for 50 years.

4.   The Government of the United Kingdom and the Government of the People's Republic of China declare that, during the transitional period between the date of the entry into force of this Joint Declaration and 30 June 1997, the Government of the United Kingdom will be responsible for the administration of Hong Kong with the object of maintaining and preserving its economic prosperity and social stability; and that the Government of the People's Republic of China will give its co-operation in this connection.

5.   The Government of the United Kingdom and the Government of the People's Republic of China declare that, in order to ensure a smooth transfer of government in 1997, and with a view to the effective implementation of this Joint Declaration, a Sino-British Joint Liaison Group will be set up when this Joint Declaration enters into force; and that it will be established and will function in accordance with the provisions of Annex II to this Joint Declaration.

6.   The Government of the United Kingdom and the Government of the People's Republic of China declare that land leases in Hong Kong and other related matters will be dealt with in accordance with the provisions of Annex III to this Joint Declaration.

7.   The Government of the United Kingdom and the Government of the People's Republic of China agree to implement the preceding declarations and the Annexes to this Joint Declaration.

8.   This Joint Declaration is subject to ratification and shall enter into force on the date of the exchange of instruments of ratification,

which shall take place in Beijing before 30 June 1985. This Joint Declaration and its Annexes shall be equally binding. . . .

For the

Government of the United
Kingdom of Great Britain
and Northern Ireland

For the

Government of the
People's Republic of
China

ANNEX I

ELABORATION BY THE GOVERNMENT OF THE PEOPLE'S REPUBLIC OF CHINA OF ITS BASIC POLICIES REGARDING HONG KONG

The Government of the People's Republic of China elaborates the basic policies of the People's Republic of China regarding Hong Kong as set out in paragraph 3 of the Joint Declaration of the Government of the United Kingdom of Great Britain and Northern Ireland and the Government of the People's Republic of China on the Question of Hong Kong as follows:

I

The Constitution of the People's Republic of China stipulates in Article 31 that 'the state may establish special administrative regions when necessary. The systems to be instituted in special administrative regions shall be prescribed by laws enacted by the National People's Congress in the light of the specific conditions'. In accordance with this Article, the People's Republic of China shall, upon the resumption of the exercise of sovereignty over Hong Kong on 1 July 1997, establish the Hong Kong Special Administrative Region of the People's Republic of China. The National People's Congress of the People's Republic of China shall enact and promulgate a Basic Law of the Hong Kong Special Administrative Region of the People's Republic of China (hereinafter referred to as the Basic Law) in accordance with the Constitution of the People's Republic of China, stipulating that after the establishment of the Hong Kong Special Administrative Region the socialist system and socialist policies shall not be practised in the Hong Kong Special Administrative Region and that Hong Kong's previous capitalist system and life-style shall remain unchanged for 50 years.

The Hong Kong Special Administrative Region shall be directly under the authority of the Central People's Government of the People's Republic of China and shall enjoy a high degree of autonomy. Except for foreign and defence affairs which are the responsibilities of the Central People's Government, the Hong Kong Special Administrative Region shall be vested with executive, legislative and independent judicial power, including that of final adjudication. The Central People's Government shall authorise the Hong Kong Special Administrative Region to conduct on its own those external affairs specified in Section XI of this Annex.

The government and legislature of the Hong Kong Special Administrative Region shall be composed of local inhabitants. The chief executive of the Hong Kong Special Administrative Region shall be selected by election or through consultations held locally and be appointed by the Central People's Government. Principal officials (equivalent to Secretaries) shall be nominated by the chief executive of the Hong Kong Special Administrative Region and appointed by the Central People's Government. The legislature of the Hong Kong Special Administrative Region shall be constituted by elections. The executive authorities shall abide by the law and shall be accountable to the legislature.

In additon to Chinese, English may also be used in organs of government and in the courts in the Hong Kong Special Administrative Region.

Apart from displaying the national flag and national emblem of the People's Republic of China, the Hong Kong Special Administrative Region may use a regional flag and emblem of its own.

II

After the establishment of the Hong Kong Special Administrative Region, the laws previously in force in Hong Kong (i.e. the common law, rules of equity, ordinances, subordinate legislation and customary law) shall be maintained, save for any that contravene the Basic Law and subject to any amendment by the Hong Kong Special Administrative Region legislature.

The legislative power of the Hong Kong Special Administrative Region shall be vested in the legislature of the Hong Kong Special Administrative Region. The legislature may on its own authority enact laws in accordance with the provisions of the Basic Law and legal procedures, and report them to the Standing Committee of the National People's Congress for the record. Laws enacted by the legislature which are in accordance with the Basic Law and legal procedures shall be regarded as valid.

The laws of the Hong Kong Special Administrative Region shall be the Basic Law, and the laws previously in force in Hong Kong and laws enacted by the Hong Kong Special Administrative Region legislature as above.

III

After the establishment of the Hong Kong Special Administrative Region, the judicial system previously practised in Hong Kong shall be maintained except for those changes consequent upon the vesting in the courts of the Hong Kong Special Administrative Region of the power of final adjudication.

Judicial power in the Hong Kong Special Administrative Region shall be vested in the courts of the Hong Kong Special Administrative Region. The courts shall exercise judicial power independently and free from any interference. Members of the judiciary shall be immune from legal action in respect of their judicial functions. The courts shall decide cases in accordance with the laws of the Hong Kong Special Administrative Region and may refer to precedents in other common law jurisdictions.

Judges of the Hong Kong Special Administrative Region courts shall be appointed by the chief executive of the Hong Kong Special Administrative Region acting in accordance with the recommendation of an independent commission composed of local judges, persons from the legal profession and other eminent persons. Judges shall be chosen by reference to their judicial qualities and may be recruited from other common law jurisdictions. A judge may only be removed for inability to discharge the functions of his office, or for misbehaviour, by the chief executive of the Hong Kong Special Administrative Region acting in accordance with the recommendation of a tribunal appointed by the chief judge of the court of final appeal, consisting of not fewer than three local judges. Additionally, the appointment or removal of principal judges (i.e. those of the highest rank) shall be made by the chief executive with the endorsement of the Hong Kong Special Administrative Region legislature and reported to the Standing Committee of the National People's Congress for the record. The system of appointment and removal of judicial officers other than judges shall be maintained.

The power of final judgment of the Hong Kong Special Administrative Region shall be vested in the court of final appeal in the Hong Kong Special Administrative Region, which may as required invite judges from other common law jurisdictions to sit on the court of final appeal.

A prosecuting authority of the Hong Kong Special Administrative Region shall control criminal prosecutions free from any interference.

On the basis of the system previously operating in Hong Kong, the Hong Kong Special Administrative Region Government shall on its own make provision for local lawyers and lawyers from outside the Hong Kong Special Administrative Region to work and practise in the Hong Kong Special Administrative Region.

The Central People's Government shall assist or authorise the Hong Kong Special Administrative Region Government to make appropriate arrangements for reciprocal juridical assistance with foreign states.

IV

After the establishment of the Hong Kong Special Administrative Region, public servants previously serving in Hong Kong in all government departments, including the police department, and members of the judiciary may all remain in employment and continue their service with pay, allowances, benefits and conditions of service no less favourable than before. The Hong Kong Special Administrative Region Government shall pay to such persons who retire or complete their contracts, as well as to those who have retired before 1 July 1997, or to their dependants, all pensions, gratuities, allowances and benefits due to them on terms no less favourable than before, and irrespective of their nationality or place of residence.

The Hong Kong Special Administrative Region Government may employ British and other foreign nationals previously serving in the public service in Hong Kong, and may recruit British and other foreign nationals holding permanent identity cards of the Hong Kong Special Administrative Region to serve as public servants at all levels, except as heads of major government departments (corresponding to branches or departments at Secretary level) including the police department, and as deputy heads of some of those departments. The Hong Kong Special Administrative Region Government may also employ British and other foreign nationals as advisers to government departments and, when there is a need, may recruit qualified candidates from outside the Hong Kong Special Administrative Region to professional and technical posts in government departments. The above shall be employed only in their individual capacities and, like other public servants, shall be responsible to the Hong Kong Special Administrative Region Government.

The appointment and promotion of public servants shall be on the basis of qualifications, experience and ability. Hong Kong's previous system of recruitment, employment, assessment, discipline, training and management for the public service (including special bodies for appointment, pay and conditions of service) shall, save for any provisions providing privileged treatment for foreign nationals, be maintained.

V

The Hong Kong Special Administrative Region shall deal on its own with financial matters, including disposing of its financial resources and drawing up its budgets and its final accounts. The Hong Kong Special Administrative Region shall report its budgets and final accounts to the Central People's Government for the record.

The Central People's Government shall not levy taxes on the Hong Kong Special Administrative Region. The Hong Kong Special Administrative Region shall use its financial revenues exclusively for its own purposes and they shall not be handed over to the Central People's Government. The systems by which taxation and public expenditure must be approved by the legislature, and by which there is accountability to the legislature for all public expenditure, and the system for auditing public accounts shall be maintained.

VI

The Hong Kong Special Administrative Region shall maintain the capitalist economic and trade systems previously practised in Hong Kong. The Hong Kong Special Administrative Region Government shall decide its economic and trade policies on its own. Rights concerning the ownership of property, including those relating to acquisition, use, disposal, inheritance and compensation for lawful deprivation (corresponding to the real value of the property concerned, freely convertible and paid without undue delay) shall continue to be protected by law.

The Hong Kong Special Administrative Region shall retain the status of a free port and continue a free trade policy, including the free movement of goods and capital. The Hong Kong Special Administrative Region may on its own maintain and develop economic and trade relations with all states and regions.

The Hong Kong Special Administrative Region shall be a separate customs territory. It may participate in relevant international organisations and international trade agreements (including preferential trade arrangements), such as the General Agreement on Tariffs and Trade and arrangements regarding international trade in textiles. Export quotas, tariff preferences and other similar arrangements obtained by the Hong Kong Special Administrative Region shall be enjoyed exclusively by the Hong Kong Special Administrative Region. The Hong Kong Special Administrative Region shall have authority to issue its own certificates of origin for products manufactured locally, in accordance with prevailing rules of origin.

The Hong Kong Special Administrative Region may, as necessary, establish official and semi-official economic and trade missions in foreign countries, reporting the establishment of such missions to the Central People's Government for the record.

VII

The Hong Kong Special Administrative Region shall retain the status of an international financial centre. The monetary and financial systems previously practised in Hong Kong, including the systems of regulation and supervision of deposit taking institutions and financial markets, shall be maintained.

The Hong Kong Special Administrative Region Government may decide its monetary and financial policies on its own. It shall safeguard the free operation of financial business and the free flow of capital within, into and out of the Hong Kong Special Administrative Region. No exchange control policy shall be applied in the Hong Kong Special Administrative Region. Markets for foreign exchange, gold, securities and futures shall continue.

The Hong Kong dollar, as the local legal tender, shall continue to circulate and remain freely convertible. The authority to issue Hong Kong currency shall be vested in the Hong Kong Special Administrative Region Government. The Hong Kong Special Administrative Region Government may authorise designated banks to issue or to continue to issue Hong Kong currency under statutory authority, after satisfying itself that any issue of currency will be soundly based and that the arrangements for such issue are consistent with the object of maintaining the stability of the currency. Hong Kong currency bearing references inappropriate to the status of Hong Kong as a Special Administrative Region of the People's Republic of China shall be progressively replaced and withdrawn from circulation.

The Exchange Fund shall be managed and controlled by the Hong Kong Special Administrative Region Government, primarily for regulating the exchange value of the Hong Kong dollar.

VIII

The Hong Kong Special Administrative Region shall maintain Hong Kong's previous systems of shipping management and shipping regulation, including the system for regulating conditions of seamen. The specific functions and responsibilities of the Hong Kong Special Administrative Region Government in the field of shipping shall be defined by the Hong Kong Special Administrative Region Government on its own. Private shipping businesses and shipping-related businesses and private container terminals in Hong Kong may continue to operate freely.

The Hong Kong Special Administrative Region shall be authorised by the Central People's Government to continue to maintain a shipping register and issue related certificates under its own legislation in the name of 'Hong Kong, China'.

With the exception of foreign warships, access for which requires the permission of the Central People's Government, ships shall enjoy access to the ports of the Hong Kong Special Administrative Region in accordance with the laws of the Hong Kong Special Administrative Region.

IX

The Hong Kong Special Administrative Region shall maintain the status of Hong Kong as a centre of international and regional aviation.

Airlines incorporated and having their principal place of business in Hong Kong and civil aviation-related businesses may continue to operate. The Hong Kong Special Administrative Region shall continue the previous system of civil aviation management in Hong Kong, and keep its own aircraft register in accordance with provisions laid down by the Central People's Government concerning nationality marks and registration marks of aircraft. The Hong Kong Special Administrative Region shall be responsible on its own for matters of routine business and technical management of civil aviation, including the management of airports, the provision of air traffic services within the flight information region of the Hong Kong Special Administrative Region, and the discharge of other responsibilities allocated under the regional air navigation procedures of the International Civil Aviation Organisation.

The Central People's Government shall, in consultation with the Hong Kong Special Administrative Region Government, make arrangements providing for air services between the Hong Kong Special Administrative Region and other parts of the People's Republic of China for airlines incorporated and having their principal place of business in the Hong Kong Special Administrative Region and other airlines of the People's Republic of China. All air service agreements providing for air services between other parts of the People's Republic of China and other states and regions with stops at the Hong Kong Special Administrative Region and air services between the Hong Kong Special Administrative Region and other states and regions with stops at other parts of the People's Republic of China shall be concluded by the Central People's Government. For this purpose, the Central People's Government shall take account of the special conditions and economic interests of the Hong Kong Special Administrative Region and consult the Hong Kong Special Administrative Region Government. Representatives of the Hong Kong Special Administrative Region Government may participate as members of delegations of the Government of the People's Republic of China in air service consultations with foreign governments concerning arrangements for such services.

Acting under specific authorisations from the Central People's Government, the Hong Kong Special Administrative Region Government may:

—renew or amend Air Service Agreements and arrangements previously in force; in principle, all such Agreements and arrangements may be renewed or amended with the rights contained in such previous Agreements and arrangements being as far as possible maintained;

—negotiate and conclude new Air Service Agreements providing routes for airlines incorporated and having their principal place of business in the Hong Kong Special Administrative Region and rights for overflights and technical stops; and

—negotiate and conclude provisional arrangements where no Air Service Agreement with a foreign state or other region is in force.

All scheduled air services to, from or through the Hong Kong Special Administrative Region which do not operate to, from or through the mainland of China shall be regulated by Air Service Agreements or provisional arrangements referred to in this paragraph.

The Central People's Government shall give the Hong Kong Special Administrative Region Government the authority to:

—negotiate and conclude with other authorities all arrangements concerning the implementation of the above Air Service Agreements and provisional arrangements;

—issue licences to airlines incorporated and having their principal place of business in the Hong Kong Special Administrative Region;

—designate such airlines under the above Air Service Agreements and provisional arrangements; and

—issue permits to foreign airlines for services other than those to, from or through the mainland of China.

X

The Hong Kong Special Administrative Region shall maintain the educational system previously practised in Hong Kong. The Hong Kong Special Administrative Region Government shall on its own decide policies in the fields of culture, education, science and technology, including policies regarding the educational system and its administration, the language of instruction, the allocation of funds, the examination system, the system of academic awards and the recognition of educational and technological qualifications. Institutions of all kinds, including those run by religious and community organisations, may retain their autonomy. They may continue to recruit staff and use teaching materials from outside the Hong Kong Special Administrative Region. Students shall enjoy freedom of choice of education and freedom to pursue their education outside the Hong Kong Special Administrative Region.

XI

Subject to the principle that foreign affairs are the responsibility of the Central People's Government, representatives of the Hong Kong Special Administrative Region Government may participate, as members of delegations of the Government of the People's Republic of China, in negotiations at the diplomatic level directly affecting the Hong Kong Special Administrative Region conducted by the Central People's Government. The Hong Kong Special Administrative Region may on its own, using the name 'Hong Kong, China', maintain and develop relations and conclude and implement agreements with states, regions and relevant international organisations in the appropriate fields, including the economic, trade, financial and monetary, shipping, communications, touristic, cultural and sporting fields. Representatives of the Hong Kong Special Administrative Region Government may participate, as members of delegations of the Government of the People's Republic of China, in international organisations or conferences in appropriate fields limited to states and affecting the Hong Kong Special Administrative Region, or may attend in such other capacity as may be permitted by the Central People's Government and the organisation or conference concerned, and may express their views in the name of 'Hong Kong, China'. The Hong Kong Special Administrative Region may, using the name 'Hong Kong, China', participate in international organisations and conferences not limited to states.

The application to the Hong Kong Special Administrative Region of international agreements to which the People's Republic of China is or becomes a party shall be decided by the Central People's Government, in accordance with the circumstances and needs of the Hong Kong Special Administrative Region, and after seeking the views of the Hong Kong Special Administrative Region Government. International agreements to which the People's Republic of China is not a party but which are implemented in Hong Kong may remain implemented in the Hong Kong Special Administrative Region. The Central People's Government shall, as necessary, authorise and assist the Hong Kong Special Administrative Region Government to make appropriate arrangements for the application to the Hong Kong Special Administrative Region of other relevant international agreements. The Central People's Government shall take the necessary steps to ensure that the Hong Kong Special Administrative Region shall continue to retain its status in an appropriate capacity in those international organisations of which the People's Republic of China is a member and in which Hong Kong participates in one capacity or another. The Central People's Government shall, where necessary, facilitate the continued participation of the Hong Kong Special Administrative Region in an appropriate capacity in those international organisations in which Hong Kong is a participant in one capacity or another, but of which the People's Republic of China is not a member.

Foreign consular and other official or semi-official missions may be established in the Hong Kong Special Administrative Region with the approval of the Central People's Government. Consular and other official missions established in Hong Kong by states which have established formal diplomatic relations with the People's Republic of China may be maintained. According to the circumstances of each case, consular and other official missions of states having no formal diplomatic relations with the People's Republic of China may either be maintained or changed to semi-official missions. States not recognised by the People's Republic of China can only establish non-governmental institutions.

The United Kingdom may establish a Consulate-General in the Hong Kong Special Administrative Region.

XII

The maintenance of public order in the Hong Kong Special Administrative Region shall be the responsibility of the Hong Kong Special Administrative Region Government. Military forces sent by the Central People's Government to be stationed in the Hong Kong Special Administrative Region for the purpose of defence shall not interfere in the internal affairs of the Hong Kong Special Administrative Region. Expenditure for these military forces shall be borne by the Central People's Government.

XIII

The Hong Kong Special Administrative Region Government shall protect the rights and freedoms of inhabitants and other persons in the Hong Kong Special Administrative Region according to law. The Hong Kong Special Administrative Region Government shall maintain the rights and freedoms as provided for by the laws previously in force in Hong Kong, including freedom of the person, of speech, of the press, of assembly, of association, to form and join trade unions, of correspondence, of travel, of movement, of strike, of demonstration, of choice of occupation, of academic research, of belief, inviolability of the home, the freedom to marry and the right to raise a family freely.

Every person shall have the right to confidential legal advice, access to the courts, representation in the courts by lawyers of his choice, and to obtain judicial remedies. Every person shall have the right to challenge the actions of the executive in the courts.

Religious organisations and believers may maintain their relations with religious organisations and believers elsewhere, and schools, hospitals and welfare institutions run by religious organisations may be continued. The relationship between religious organisations in the Hong Kong Special Administrative Region and those in other parts of the People's Republic of China shall be based on the principles of non-subordination, non-interference and mutual respect.

The provisions of the International Covenant on Civil and Political Rights and the International Covenant on Economic, Social and Cultural Rights as applied to Hong Kong shall remain in force.

XIV

The following categories of persons shall have the right of abode in the Hong Kong Special Administrative Region, and, in accordance with the law of the Hong Kong Special Administrative Region, be qualified to obtain permanent identity cards issued by the Hong Kong Special Administrative Region Government, which state their right of abode:

—all Chinese nationals who were born or who have ordinarily resided in Hong Kong before or after the establishment of the Hong Kong Special Administrative Region for a continuous period of seven years or more, and persons of Chinese nationality born outside Hong Kong of such Chinese nationals;

—all other persons who have ordinarily resided in Hong Kong before or after the establishment of the Hong Kong Special Administrative Region for a continuous period of seven years or more and who have taken Hong Kong as their place of permanent residence before or after the establishment of the Hong Kong Special Administrative Region, and persons under 21 years of age who were born of such persons in Hong Kong before or after the establishment of the Hong Kong Special Administrative Region;

—any other persons who had the right of abode only in Hong Kong before the establishment of the Hong Kong Special Administrative Region.

The Central People's Government shall authorise the Hong Kong Special Administrative Region Government to issue, in accordance with the law, passports of the Hong Kong Special Administrative Region of the People's Republic of China to all Chinese nationals who hold permanent identity cards of the Hong Kong Special Administrative Region, and travel documents of the Hong Kong Special Administrative Region of the People's Republic of China to all other persons lawfully residing in the Hong Kong Special Administrative Region. The above passports and documents shall be valid for all states and regions and shall record the holder's right to return to the Hong Kong Special Administrative Region.

For the purpose of travelling to and from the Hong Kong Special Administrative Region, residents of the Hong Kong Special Administrative Region may use travel documents issued by the Hong Kong Special Administrative Region Government, or by other competent authorities of the People's Republic of China, or of other states. Holders of permanent identity cards of the Hong Kong Special Administrative Region may have this fact stated in their travel documents as evidence that the holders have the right of abode in the Hong Kong Special Administrative Region.

Entry into the Hong Kong Special Administrative Region of persons from other parts of China shall continue to be regulated in accordance with the present practice.

The Hong Kong Special Administrative Region Government may apply immigration controls on entry, stay in and departure from the Hong Kong Special Administrative Region by persons from foreign states and regions.

Unless restrained by law, holders of valid travel documents shall be free to leave the Hong Kong Special Administrative Region without special authorisation.

The Central People's Government shall assist or authorise the Hong Kong Special Administrative Region Government to conclude visa abolition agreements with states or regions.

ANNEX II

SINO-BRITISH JOINT LIAISON GROUP

1.   In furtherance of their common aim and in order to ensure a smooth transfer of government in 1997, the Government of the United Kingdom and the Government of the People's Republic of China have agreed to continue their discussions in a friendly spirit and to develop the co-operative relationship which already exists between the two Governments over Hong Kong with a view to the effective implementation of the Joint Declaration.

2.   In order to meet the requirements for liaison, consultation and the exchange of information, the two Governments have agreed to set up a Joint Liaison Group.

3.   The functions of the Joint Liaison Group shall be:

(a) to conduct consultations on the implementation of the Joint Declaration;

(b) to discuss matters relating to the smooth transfer of government in 1997;

(c) to exchange information and conduct consultations on such subjects as may be agreed by the two sides.

Matters on which there is disagreement in the Joint Liaison Group shall be referred to the two Governments for solution through consultations.

4.   Matters for consideration during the first half of the period between the establishment of the Joint Liaison Group and 1 July 1997 shall include:

(a) action to be taken by the two Governments to enable the Hong Kong Special Administrative Region to maintain its economic relations as a separate customs territory, and in particular to ensure the maintenance of Hong Kong's participation in the

General Agreement on Tariffs and Trade, the Multifibre Arrangement and other international arrangements; and

(b) action to be taken by the two Governments to ensure the continued application of international rights and obligations affecting Hong Kong.

5.   The two Governments have agreed that in the second half of the period between the establishment of the Joint Liaison Group and 1 July 1997 there will be need for closer co-operation, which will therefore be intensified during that period. Matters for consideration during this second period shall include:

(a) procedures to be adopted for the smooth transition in 1997;

(b) action to assist the Hong Kong Special Administrative Region to maintain and develop economic and cultural relations and conclude agreements on these matters with states, regions and relevant international organisations.

6.   The Joint Liaison Group shall be an organ for liasion and not an organ of power. It shall play no part in the administration of Hong Kong or the Hong Kong Special Administrative Region. Nor shall it have any supervisory role over that administration. The members and supporting staff of the Joint Liaison Group shall only conduct activities within the scope of the functions of the Joint Liaison Group.

7.   Each side shall designate a senior representative, who shall be of Ambassadorial rank, and four other members of the group. Each side may send up to 20 supporting staff.

8.   The Joint Liaison Group shall be established on the entry into force of the Joint Declaration. From 1 July 1988 the Joint Liaison Group shall have its principal base in Hong Kong. The Joint Liaison Group shall continue its work until 1 January 2000.

9.   The Joint Liaison Group shall meet in Beijing, London and Hong Kong. It shall meet at least once in each of the three locations in

each year. The venue for each meeting shall be agreed between the two sides.

10. Members of the Joint Liaison Group shall enjoy diplomatic privileges and immunities as appropriate when in the three locations. Proceedings of the Joint Liaison Group shall remain confidential unless otherwise agreed between the two sides.

11. The Joint Liaison Group may by agreement between the two sides decide to set up specialist sub-groups to deal with particular subjects requiring expert assistance.

12. Meetings of the Joint Liaison Group and sub-groups may be attended by experts other than the members of the Joint Liaison Group. Each side shall determine the composition of its delegation to particular meetings of the Joint Liaison Group or sub-group in accordance with the subjects to be discussed and the venue chosen.

13. The working procedures of the Joint Liaison Group shall be discussed and decided upon by the two sides within the guidelines laid down in this Annex.

ANNEX III

LAND LEASES

The Government of the United Kingdom and the Government of the People's Republic of China have agreed that, with effect from the entry into force of the Joint Declaration, land leases in Hong Kong and other related matters shall be dealt with in accordance with the following provisions:

1. All leases of land granted or decided upon before the entry into force of the Joint Declaration and those granted thereafter in accordance with paragraph 2 or 3 of this Annex, and which extend beyond 30 June 1977, and all rights in relation to such leases shall continue to be recognised and protected under the law of the Hong Kong Special Administrative Region.

2.   All leases of land granted by the British Hong Kong Government not containing a right of renewal that expire before 30 June 1997, except short-term tenancies and leases for special purposes, may be extended if the lessee so wishes for a period expiring not later than 30 June 2047 without payment of an additional premium. An annual rent shall be charged from the date of extension equivalent to 3 per cent of the rateable value of the property at that date, adjusted in step with any changes in the rateable value thereafter. In the case of old schedule lots, village lots, small houses and similar rural holdings, where the property was on 30 June 1984 held by, or, in the case of small houses granted after that date, the property is granted to, a person descended through the male line from a person who was in 1898 a resident of an established village in Hong Kong, the rent shall remain unchanged so long as the property is held by that person or by one of his lawful successors in the male line. Where leases of land not having a right of renewal expire after 30 June 1997, they shall be dealt with in accordance with the relevant land laws and policies of the Hong Kong Special Administrative Region.

3.   From the entry into force of the Joint Declaration until 30 June 1997, new leases of land may be granted by the British Hong Kong Government for terms expiring not later than 30 June 2047. Such leases shall be granted at a premium and nominal rental until 30 June 1997, after which date they shall not require payment of an additional premium but an annual rent equivalent to 3 per cent of the rateable value of the property at that date, adjusted in step with changes in the rateable value thereafter, shall be charged.

4.   The total amount of new land to be granted under paragraph 3 of this Annex shall be limited to 50 hectares a year (excluding land to be granted to the Hong Kong Housing Authority for public rental housing) from the entry into force of the Joint Declaration until 30 June 1997.

5.   Modifications of the conditions specified in leases granted by the British Hong Kong Government may continue to be granted before 1 July 1997 at a premium equivalent to the difference between the value

of the land under the previous conditions and its value under the modified conditions.

6. From the entry into force of the Joint Declaration until 30 June 1997, premium income obtained by the British Hong Kong Government from land transactions shall, after deduction of the average cost of land production, be shared equally between the British Hong Kong Government and the future Hong Kong Special Administrative Region Government. All the income obtained by the British Hong Kong Government, including the amount of the abovementioned deduction, shall be put into the Capital Works Reserve Fund for the financing of land development and public works in Hong Kong. The Hong Kong Special Administrative Region Government's share of the premium income shall be deposited in banks incorporated in Hong Kong and shall not be drawn on except for the financing of land development and public works in Hong Kong in accordance with the provisions of paragraph 7(d) of this Annex.

7. A Land Commission shall be established in Hong Kong immediately upon the entry into force of the Joint Declaration. The Land Commission shall be composed of an equal number of officials designated respectively by the Government of the United Kingdom and the Government of the People's Republic of China together with necessary supporting staff. The officials of the two sides shall be responsible to their respective governments. The Land Commission shall be dissolved on 30 June 1997.

The terms of reference of the Land Commission shall be:

(a) to conduct consultations on the implementation of this Annex;

(b) to monitor observance of the limit specified in paragraph 4 of this Annex, the amount of land granted to the Hong Kong Housing Authority for public rental housing, and the division and use of premium income referred to in paragraph 6 of this Annex;

(c) to consider and decide on proposals from the British Hong Kong Government for increasing the limit referred to in paragraph 4 of this Annex;

(d) to examine proposals for drawing on the Hong Kong Special Administrative Region Government's share of premium income referred to in paragraph 6 of this Annex and to make recommendations to the Chinese side for decision.

Matters on which there is disagreement in the Land Commission shall be referred to the Government of the United Kingdom and the Government of the People's Republic of China for decision.

8. Specific details regarding the establishment of the Land Commission shall be finalised separately by the two sides through consultations.

EXCHANGE OF MEMORANDA

(a) UNITED KINGDOM MEMORANDUM

MEMORANDUM

In connection with the Joint Declaration of the Government of the United Kingdom of Great Britain and Northern Ireland and the Government of the People's Republic of China on the question of Hong Kong to be signed this day, the Government of the United Kingdom declares that, subject to the completion of the necessary amendments to the relevant United Kingdom legislation:

(a) All persons who on 30 June 1997 are, by virtue of a connection with Hong Kong, British Dependent Territories citizens (BDTCs) under the law in force in the United Kingdom will cease to be BDTCs with effect from 1 July 1997, but will be eligible to retain an appropriate status which, without conferring the right of abode in the United Kingdom, will entitle them to continue to use passports issued by the Government of the United Kingdom. This status will be acquired by such persons only if they hold or are included in such a British passport issued before 1 July 1997, except that eligible persons born on or after 1 January 1997 but before 1 July 1997 may obtain or be included in such a passport up to 31 December 1997.

(b) No person will acquire BDTC status on or after 1 July 1997 by virtue of a connection with Hong Kong. No person born on or after 1 July 1997 will acquire the status referred to as being appropriate in sub-paragraph (a).

(c) United Kingdom consular officials in the Hong Kong Special Administrative Region and elsewhere may renew and replace passports of persons mentioned in sub-paragraph (a) and may also issue them to persons, born before 1 July 1997 of such persons, who had previously been included in the passport of their parent.

(d) Those who have obtained or been included in passports issued by the Government of the United Kingdom under sub-paragraphs (a) and (c) will be entitled to receive, upon request, British consular services and protection when in third countries.

Beijing, 1984.

(b) CHINESE MEMORANDUM

MEMORANDUM

Translation

The Government of the People's Republic of China has received the memorandum from the Government of the United Kingdom of Great Britain and Northern Ireland dated 1984.

Under the Nationality Law of the People's Republic of China, all Hong Kong Chinese compatriots, whether they are holders of the 'British Dependent Territories citizens' Passport' or not, are Chinese nationals.

Taking account of the historical background of Hong Kong and its realities, the competent authorities of the Government of the People's Republic of China will, with effect from 1 July 1997, permit Chinese nationals in Hong Kong who were previously called 'British Dependent Territories citizens' to use travel documents issued by the Government of the United Kingdom for the purpose of travelling to other states and regions.

The above Chinese nationals will not be entitled to British consular protection in the Hong Kong Special Administrative Region and other parts of the People's Republic of China on account of their holding the above-mentioned British travel documents.

Beijing, 1984.

Printed in the UK for HMSO.
Dd294181   c30   7/92